My little
Bullet
Book

Be gorgeously organized

David Sinden

FLATIRON
BOOKS
NEW YORK

To Sandrina

MY LITTLE BULLET BOOK. Copyright © 2017 by David Sinden.
All rights reserved. Printed in the United States of America. For information,
address Flatiron Books, 175 Fifth Avenue, New York, N.Y. 10010.

www.flatironbooks.com

The Library of Congress Cataloging-in-Publication Data
is available upon request

ISBN 978-1-250-17127-6 (trade paperback)

Our books may be purchased in bulk for promotional, educational,
or business use. Please contact your local bookseller or the
Macmillan Corporate and Premium Sales Department at
1-800-221-7945, extension 5442, or by email at
MacmillanSpecialMarkets@macmillan.com.

Originally published in the UK by Bluebird, an imprint of Pan Macmillan

First U.S. Edition: September 2017

10 9 8 7 6 5 4 3 2 1

this belongs to

Create
the life
YOU want

Organize your World around your Dreams and watch them come TRUE

What is
My Little Bullet Book?

<u>My Little Bullet Book</u> is your indispensible companion. In one handy volume, it takes the place of a diary, scratch pad, life coach, personal assistant and planner. It will help you gain a bigger picture of your priorities and purpose as well as provide a place for you to tackle tasks, achieve goals and plan your monthly and weekly schedules. Use it to keep track of your finances, contacts and habits, and discover methods and exercises to help you create a fulfilled life. There is no need to begin in January: unlike a diary <u>My Little Bullet Book</u> is ready to start on any day of the year you choose. So begin now; be gorgeously organized and create the life you want.

❀   ❀   ❀

Tip: Use a pencil throughout. Buy yourself a nice one—perhaps a retractable pencil that stays sharp. This will allow you to alter and update your <u>Little Bullet Book</u> at any time.

Contents

Personalize

Begin by personalizing your <u>Little Bullet Book</u>. Starting with the current month, write the names of the upcoming twelve months into your "Yearly me" and "Monthly me" pages—this will provide you with a yearly schedule from today.

Explore the personal exercises throughout to review your life and advance your fulfillment.

Use the "Task tracker" pages to organize your tasks, the "My piggy bank" pages to work out your money and budgets, and the "More me" pages to expand on anything specific to you. Finally, the "Weekly schedule and personal notes" section offers space for your weekly appointments when required or for weekly development practices—update the Contents pages with any additions you make so you can find your entries in an instant.

❀   ❀   ❀

"Anticipate the difficult by managing the easy" —Jane Austen

～ My bullets ～

Tracking tasks and goals on paper helps clear your mind. All half-finished tasks and goals are open loops that the mind won't let go of, plus marking tasks "done" creates pleasure sensations in the brain, reducing anxiety.

You may like to create your own set of customized bullet points when keeping track of tasks. Here is a suggested set of bullet points, though feel free to add to these or to adopt any method that works for you.

○ To do

⊙ Incomplete

⊗ Urgent

⊖ Delegate

● Done/canceled

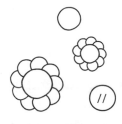

Life overview

Evaluating and organizing your life will not only keep you up to date but will help you gain a bigger picture of your goals, priorities and purpose, bringing to light areas of your life in which you are advancing.

Using your Wheel of balance, shade your current life-overview as you see it, scoring each area of your life between 1 and 10.

Wheel of balance

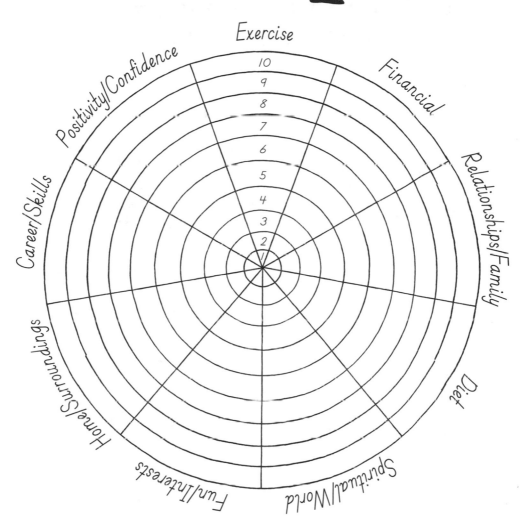

Exercise

Financial

Relationships/Family

Diet

Spiritual/World

Fun/Interests

Home/Surroundings

Career/Skills

Positivity/Confidence

Look back to this page from time to time to see what might have changed.

Yearly me

Label each month. Bullet notes for the year ahead.
Transfer relevant info to your "Monthly me" pages.

month 1

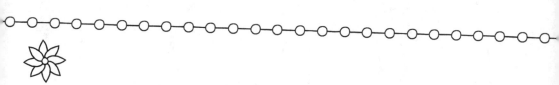

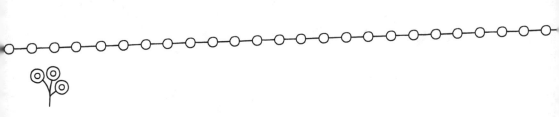

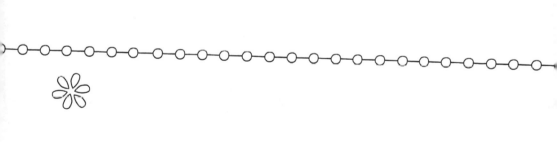

"What you are comes to you"
—Ralph Waldo Emerson

16

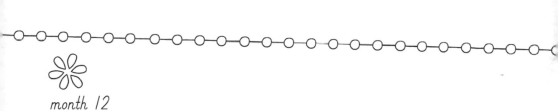

month 12

"The past, the present and the future are really one: they are today" —Harriet Beecher Stowe

Monthly me

insert month

✓ This month's key goals, projects and commitments in bullet points.

"The secret of getting ahead is getting started" —Mark Twain

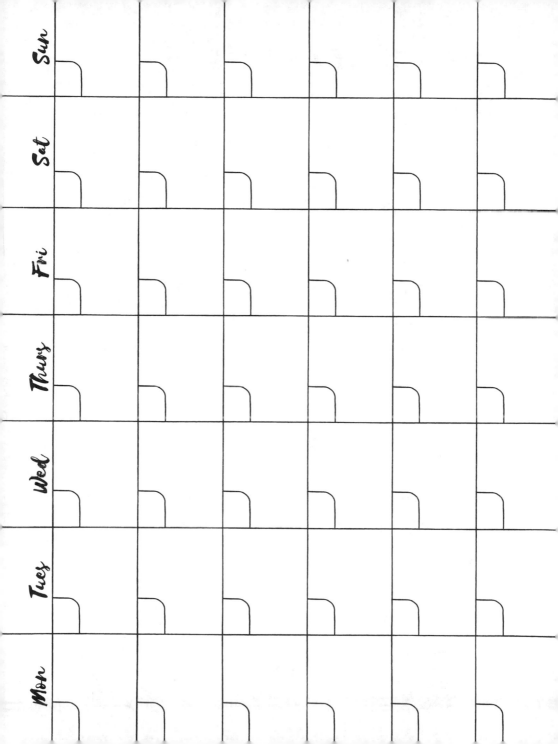

Tackling tasks

Remember: you are not the servant of your to-do list; it exists to serve you. Write down tasks that need doing. Label them by type, e.g. P for phone calls, O for online, and, when possible, tackle a few of the same type together for efficiency.

If a task takes less than two minutes, do it now.
If a task can be delegated, delegate it.
For large tasks, tackle only the next required action.

Always focus on your desired outcome from a task, not the task itself. There may be several tasks on your list connected to the same outcome, such as get fit or improve my social life. When all is said and done, the outcome is what matters, and this can be achieved in numerous ways—listing endless details is distracting, not useful. Focus on the desired outcome and only then begin— you will instantly find that by remaining outcome-

focused rather than task-focused, solutions materialize faster.

Before diving in to your tasks, prioritize them by asking yourself how important and how urgent each one is. Use the system below to help you focus your time and energy effectively. In which of the four categories does each task belong?

&	Important	Not Important
Urgent	1 Do these tasks.	2 These tasks may be demands made on you that need delegating or saying "no" to.
Not Urgent	3 Never neglect these tasks. They are likely the things you care about that will affect your goals and dreams.	4 Ignore these tasks. They are pointless distractions.

"We can't all do everything" —Virgil

Task tracker

Keep track of tasks that need doing. Update their status using your personalized bullet symbols. Cross tasks off when completed or out of date. Move ongoing tasks to your next Task tracker.

Date	Type	Status	Task
		○	
		○	
		○	
		○	
		○	
		○	
		○	
		○	
		○	
		○	
		○	
		○	
		○	
		○	
		○	
		○	
		○	
		○	
		○	

"Let your performance do the thinking"
—Charlotte Brontë

My goals for a better life balance

Date / /

Exercise
○ ....

Financial
○ ....

Relationships / Family
○ ....

Diet
○ ....

Spiritual / World
○ ....

Fun / Interests
○ ....

Home / Surroundings
○ ....

Career / Skills
○ ....

Positivity / Confidence
○ ....

～ Day planner ～

Date / /

Goals

To do

Meals

B
L
D
S

Exercise

Social/Fun/Leisure

Key timings

Notes

25

Personal project Date / /

To tackle projects like a pro, use outcome planning.
Simply create a clear vision of the desired outcome
in your life that you see this project bringing you.
Now pursue and prioritize that outcome.

Project:

Intended outcome:

Thoughts:

Next action required:

Research

"I have not failed. I've just found 10,000 ways that won't work" —Thomas A. Edison

Enjoying myself

Bullet what you've enjoyed, recently and past.

○
○
○
○
○
○
○
○
○
○
○
○
○

○
○
○
○
○
○
○
○
○
○
○
○
○
○
○
○

Now check your lifestyle and your schedule—be sure to include these things in it.

Time has a **WONDERFUL** *WAY* of showing us what **REALLY** matters

29

My piggy bank

Date / /

Money buys me amusement,
not happiness

~ Beautiful me ~

Goals, self-care and products to try:

Monthly me

"The two most powerful warriors are patience and time" —Leo Tolstoy

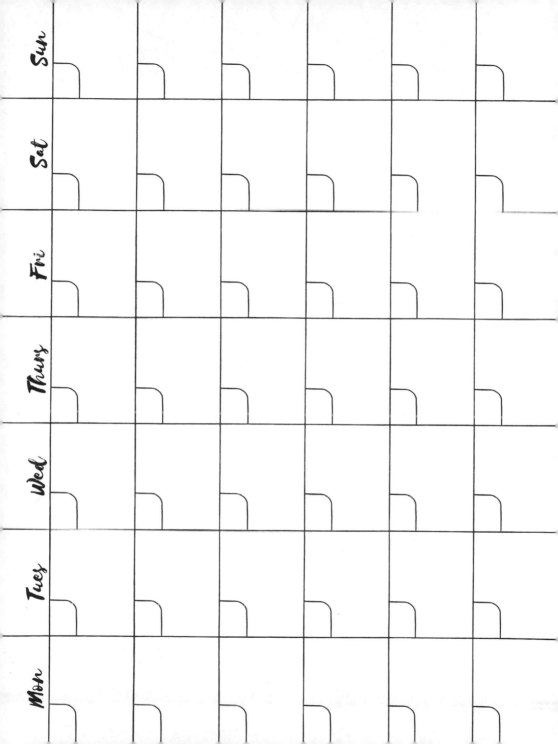

Task tracker

Date	Type	Status	Task
		○	
		○	
		○	
		○	
		○	
		○	
		○	
		○	
		○	
		○	
		○	
		○	
		○	
		○	
		○	
		○	
		○	
		○	
		○	
		○	
		○	

"Arrange whatever pieces come your way"
—Virginia Woolf

Home improvements

"There is nothing like staying at home for real comfort" —Jane Austen

Be willing to minimize all that you own. More things bring more problems—more upkeep, more to clean, more to store, more to think about—and they hide the meaningful items. Rule of thumb: if you don't love it or it isn't useful, get rid of it. Start now:

Out of clutter, find simplicity

My personal trainer

Plan or track your exercise.

Highlight your reasons for exercising to keep them in mind.

- Reduce body fat ○ Increase flexibility
- Increase aerobic power ○ Better circulation
- Healthy immune function ○ Tone muscles
- Improve breathing ○ Lower blood pressure
- Lower Type-2 diabetes risk. ○ Improve sex life
- Look good naked ○ Boost energy ○ Sleep better
- Reduce anxiety ○ Improve thinking ○ Fun

Create a vision of yourself having achieved the physical goal you desire. How do you look and feel? Have you lost weight or gained strength? See it vividly. A vision pulls us toward achieving our goals more effectively than willpower can push us.

....

....

....

....

....

"Every action needs to be prompted by a motive" —Leonardo da Vinci

I am what I eat

Plan healthy adjustments to your diet.

What goes into your body accounts for the fluids in which every cell of your body bathes. For one day, or one week, honestly monitor your meals, drinks and snacks:

When a fish is sick, first change its water

~ My friends, family and causes ~

Give to others—remember gifts and birthday dates.

"No one has ever become poor from giving" —Anne Frank

My affirmations

Repeating daily affirmations can positively alter your subconscious thinking. Keep affirmations specific and phrase them as if they are already so. Construct them in the positive: exclude words like "not" or "won't." e.g. "I am healthy and sugar free," rather than "I will not eat sugar."

"Mind moves matter" —Virgil

My piggy bank

Date / /

"The first wealth is health"

—Ralph Waldo Emerson

Me-time

"Trust in dreams, for in them is hidden the gate to eternity" —Kahlil Gibran

Monthly me

"If you do not change direction you may
end up where you are heading" —Lao Tzu

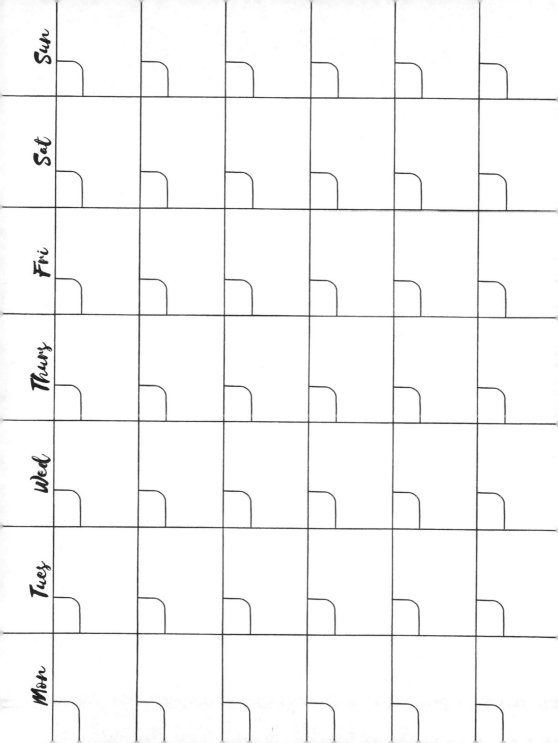

Task tracker

Date	Type	Status	Task
		○	
		○	
		○	
		○	
		○	
		○	
		○	
		○	
		○	
		○	
		○	
		○	
		○	
		○	
		○	
		○	
		○	
		○	
		○	
		○	
		○	
		○	

"I want to do it because I want to do it"
—Amelia Earhart

My mission

Creating a personal mission helps to focus and organize your life in line with your nature, values and priorities. Your mission acts as the blueprint for choosing your goals and actions. Take time to answer these questions personally and honestly—this is for you:

When have I felt energized?

What are my strengths and talents?

What character traits do I admire in others?

What and whom do I care about?

What are my passions or interests?

When have I felt enjoyment?

What life would I create with a magic wand?

What could I do for others or the world?

What do my surroundings look like when I think of myself feeling content?

How would I live if I believed that money was not important?

Look back on your answers. Pick out key traits and themes that speak to you about the person you wish to be and the values you wish to live by. Combine these into a personal mission statement expressing your intent going forward. Write it in pencil on the next page to refer to when organizing your life, or to develop when necessary.

Here are two examples of personal mission statements:

My personal mission is to live honestly and compassionately, and to cherish my health, family and the environment. I wish to actively care about nature and to engage physically with the world.

My personal mission is to grow spiritually and creatively; to seek opportunities for an artistic and altruistic life. I wish to be inventive and kind, for myself and others, and willing to take a risk.

"This above all; to thine own self be true" —William Shakespeare

My personal
mission statement

....

....

....

....

....

....

....

....

....

....

....

....

Date / /

Wardrobe detox

Without looking, try to bring to mind the clothes you own. Note the items that you <u>love</u> to wear.

Now check in your wardrobe. Anything you did not note, more than likely should be ditched. Give it to charity. If an item doesn't fit well, do the same. These items are all weighing you down. Keep fewer and you'll look and feel better.

Books to read. Music to listen to. Films to see.

○
○
○
○
○
○
○
○
○
○
○
○
○
○

○
○
○
○
○
○
○
○
○
○
○
○
○
○

"Books, like friends, should be few and well-chosen" —Samuel Johnson

My piggy bank

Date / /

Money buys me clothes,
not style

Me-time

"**The sun is new each day**" —*Heraclitus*

Monthly me

"To be is to do" —Immanuel Kant

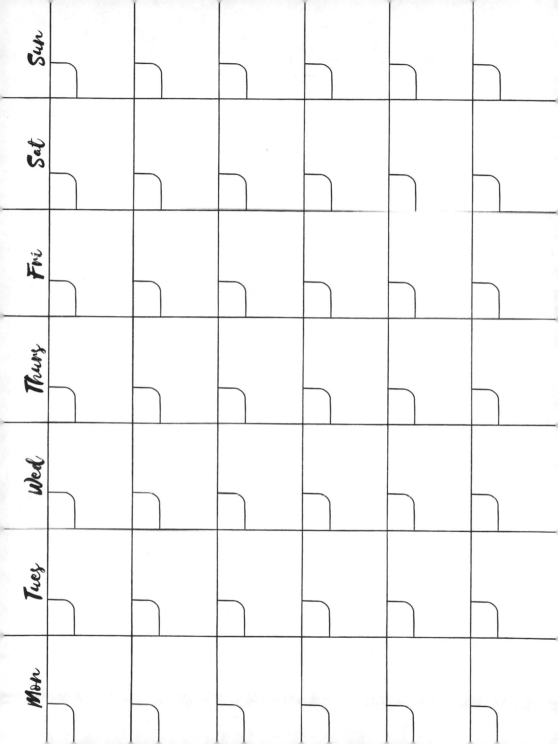

Task tracker

Date	Type	Status	Task
		○	
		○	
		○	
		○	
		○	
		○	
		○	
		○	
		○	
		○	
		○	
		○	
		○	
		○	
		○	
		○	
		○	
		○	
		○	
		○	
		○	
		○	
		○	

"Self-development is a higher duty than self-sacrifice" —Elizabeth Cady Stanton

Challenges

An essential part of a rich, fulfilled life is to feel regularly challenged. When we challenge ourselves we grow and gain confidence. This is critical for experiencing progress.

A challenge should be something that feels a little different or even daunting. It can be big or small. Even small challenges have an impact on our lives.

Challenges are not the same as goals. They are new experiences or approaches that will open fresh mindsets and beliefs. For instance, "I'll attend that seminar out of curiosity," "I'll avoid television all week," "I'll book that trip regardless."

Commit to regular challenges, big or small. They will reveal qualities you didn't know you had, change your perceptions of what is normal or achievable, and break any limiting beliefs you have about yourself. Your self-esteem and connection to the world will increase, and you will have richer experiences.

Personal challenges to try:

○
○
○
○
○
○
○
○
○
○
○
○
○
○
○
○
○
○
○
○

Don't limit your challenges. Challenge your limits

Spoiling myself

Keep a wishlist of things you'd like to receive
(or could treat yourself to).

my
Sleep
monitor

Track the sleep you're getting. Is it regular? Can you improve your sleep habits or bedtime rituals?

"A well-spent day brings happy sleep" —Leonardo da Vinci

My pursuits

Plan or track an interest or hobby, or find information on a new one.

"Curiosity is . . . the first passion and the last" —William Samuel Johnson

My piggy bank

Date / /

"The price of anything is the amount of life you exchange for it" —Henry David Thoreau

Me-time

"Whatever you are, be a good one"

—Abraham Lincoln

Monthly me

"Better three hours too soon than a minute too late" —William Shakespeare

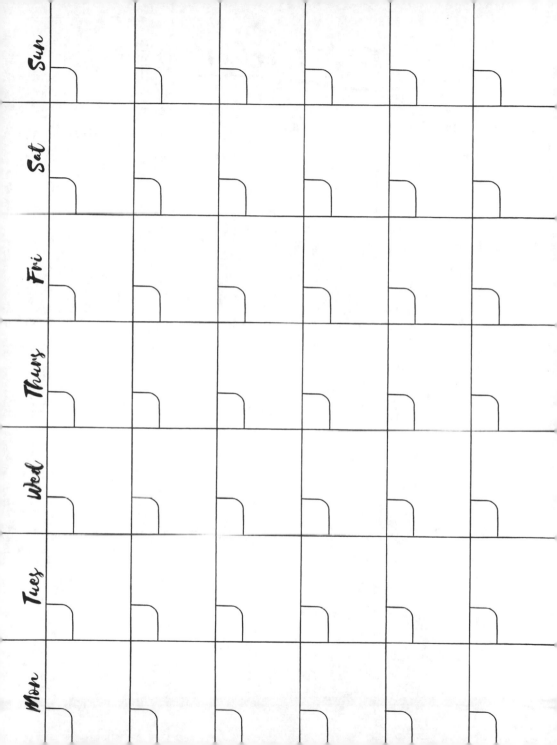

Task tracker

Date	Type	Status	Task
		○	
		○	
		○	
		○	
		○	
		○	
		○	
		○	
		○	
		○	
		○	
		○	
		○	
		○	
		○	
		○	
		○	
		○	
		○	
		○	
		○	
		○	

"Well begun is half done" —Aristotle

Beliefs

Of all the things that hinder or help us to create the life we want, beliefs have perhaps the most impact. In general, what we beleive about ourselves and the world is pretty much what we get. But our beliefs can be out of date or untrue, and limit us. They may relate to how we thought as a child, have come out of an isolated experience or have been adopted from someone else.

When we throw out limiting beliefs and replace them with helpful ones we open up new possibilities. Being oneself does not mean being rigid and never evolving. Whatever beliefs you hold, if they limit you, update them. Beliefs form part of our subconscious, which has a big impact on how we live. Examine the beliefs you hold. Are they all completely true? Is each working for you or limiting you?

"Whether you think you can or can't, you're right" —Henry Ford

Isolate a belief and say it out loud:
e.g. "I'm not an artistic or creative person."

....

....

What could be the root of this belief?
e.g. At school I found it tricky to draw and left Art
behind as a subject.

....

....

How is this limiting me?
e.g. I rarely explore creative interests or pleasures.

....

....

Create an updated belief.
e.g. I welcome trying new artistic opportunities and
acquiring new creative skills beyond drawing.

....

....

Acknowledge the old belief as redundant. Cement the
new one by writing it as an affirmation, visualizing it
and actioning it in your challenges.

Belief ○

Root ○

 Limits ○

Update it ○

 Belief ○

Root ○

 Limits ○

Update it ○

 Belief ○

Root ○

 Limits ○

Update it ○

 "If the Sun and Moon should ever doubt, they'd immediately go out" —William Blake

— Create a new habit —

Our little habits are what make or break our big ambitions, and they are born from our self-image. For instance, if you view yourself as health-conscious, you'll be more likely to eat a low-sugar cereal for breakfast than a chocolate-chip muffin. Whatever we identify with, we achieve with ease. Bullet new habits you would like to embrace.

○

○

○

○

○

Pick a manageable one, and adopt an appropriate view of yourself that supports it. For seven days follow through on the habit as part of your identity.

M T W T F S S

○ ○ ○ ○ ○ ○ ○

"Habits change into character" —Ovid

I am grateful for . . .

To create an abundant life, start from the inside and work your way out, by expressing gratitude for everything you already have. Regularly bullet what you are grateful for:

○
○
○
○
○
○
○
○
○
○
○
○
○
○
○
○
○

○
○
○
○
○
○
○
○
○
○
○
○
○
○
○
○
○

- ◯
- ◯
- ◯
- ◯
- ◯
- ◯
- ◯
- ◯
- ◯
- ◯
- ◯
- ◯
- ◯
- ◯
- ◯
- ◯
- ◯
- ◯
- ◯
- ◯

"Gratitude is not only the greatest of virtues, but the parent of all the others" —Marcus Tullius Cicero

My piggy bank

Date / /

Money buys me technology, not brains

Me-time

"When I give, I give myself" —Walt Whitman

Monthly me

"Be happy for this moment.
This moment is your life" —Omar Khayyam

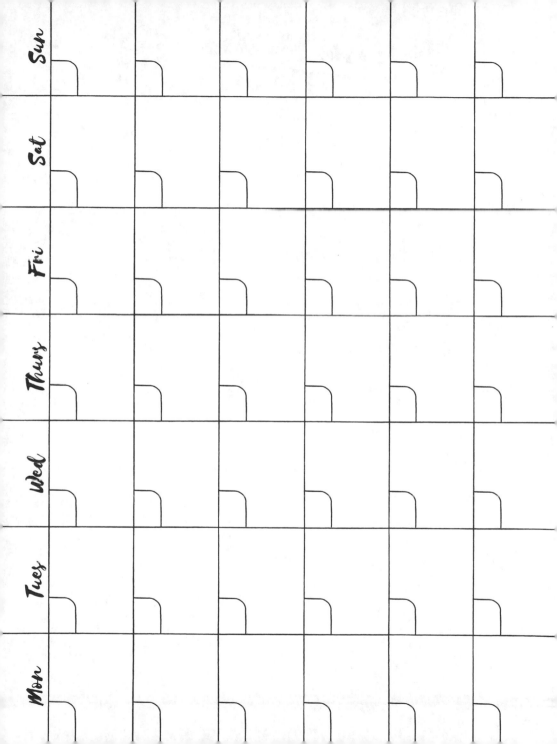

Task tracker

Date	Type	Status	Task
		○	
		○	
		○	
		○	
		○	
		○	
		○	
		○	
		○	
		○	
		○	
		○	
		○	
		○	
		○	
		○	
		○	
		○	
		○	
		○	
		○	
		○	
		○	

"I attribute my success to this — I never gave or took any excuse" —Florence Nightingale

~ Law of attraction ~

The law of attraction is the belief that we attract into our lives more of whatever we focus on. For instance, if we would like a different job, relationship or to be free of debt, the law of attraction suggests to move our thoughts wholly away from the things that are wrong with our current job, relationship or debt, as not doing so will only attract more of the same problems. Instead, we must focus specifically and positively on what we do want. Visualize it, then start believing we have it or that it is coming to us. Behave as if it is so. Manifesting in this way switches our thoughts, actions and speech to the right energy to attract what we desire. Combined with healthy values and a flexible attitude, manifesting your deisires and believing you can achieve them, quite simply directs life wholeheartedly in that direction.

Thoughts become things

Write what you wish to attract:

Let go and act as if it is already so.
Know it is on its way. Behave as if you have it.

Create an affirmation expressing yourself having it:

Visualize yourself experiencing it:

Practical actions to take now to assist it;
be proactive and flexible:

Look for opportunities. Like attracts like.
You receive what you believe.

Places to visit

"Explore. Dream. Discover"

—Mark Twain

 # Travel planner

To pack:

Details and contacts:

Passport no.:
Vaccinations log:

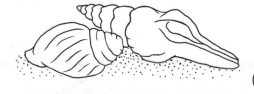

Health check-ups

Track appointments and body matters.

✿ Refresh myself

Three new things I am grateful for:

○ ....

○ ....

○ ....

Two life areas I am improving:

○ ....

○ ....

Three new affirmations or beliefs:

○ ....

○ ....

○ ....

Two current goals:

○ ....

○ ....

One current challenge:

○ ....

"All things great are bound up with all little things" —Lucy Maud Montgomery

My piggy bank

Date / /

"Poor and content is rich and rich enough" —William Shakespeare

Me-time

"Let the beauty of what you love be what you do" —Rumi

Monthly me

"Perfection is attained by slow degrees;
it requires the hand of time" —Voltaire

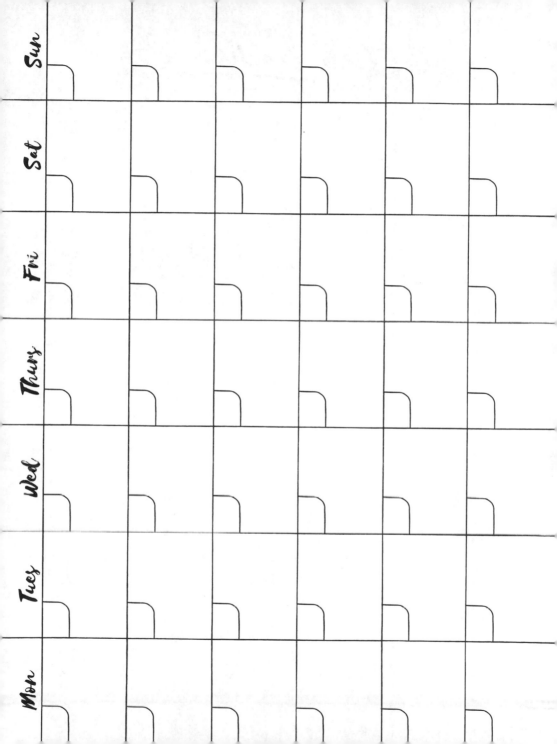

Task tracker

Date	Type	Status	Task
		◯	
		◯	
		◯	
		◯	
		◯	
		◯	
		◯	
		◯	
		◯	
		◯	
		◯	
		◯	
		◯	
		◯	
		◯	
		◯	
		◯	
		◯	
		◯	
		◯	
		◯	
		◯	

"To begin, begin" —William Wordsworth

Visualize goals

Visualizing goals or wants is a powerful and effective way of achieving them or attracting them to your life. The subconscious does not distinguish between a lived experience and a visualized experience. If you shut your eyes and visualize stepping to the edge of a cliff, you will feel a physical reaction to this, even though it is only in your mind's eye.

Use the powerful tool of visualization to focus your subconscious on the things that you desire. Once you do, your subconscious will work for you twenty-four hours a day in pursuit of them.

You can do this by taking time out to sit quietly, picturing things in your mind. Or, equally as effective, you can create a vision board. Treat your vision board like a scrapbook page. Add images that convey the accomplishment of your goals and desires. Search the internet, magazines and your own paperwork. Create a vision board of someone you want to meet, or something you want to accomplish or attain.

My vision board

The subconscious mind seeks out ways and
means that the conscious mind cannot plan

What do I want?

Bullet the things you want next in life, expressing yourself only in the positive.

○

○

○

○

○

○

○

○

○

○

○

○

Now consider this list in relation to your personal mission statement—what do you really want? What will have the greatest impact?

"The mind enamoured with deceptive things, declines things better" —Horace

Maybe so, maybe not. We'll see.

During wartime, when food was scarce, a farmer had one horse to plow his whole farm. One night, the horse ran off, and in the morning the farmer's son discovered its stable empty. "Our horse is gone! This is terrible!" he cried.

The farmer replied, "Maybe so, maybe not. We'll see."

Days later, the horse returned accompanied by another. The boy excitedly called, "Look, it's back! And we have two horses now! This is great news!"

The farmer replied, "Maybe so, maybe not. We'll see."

The next week, the farmer's son was trying to plow with the new horse when it trampled him, breaking his leg. Unable to work, he was forced to rest. "This is the worst luck ever!"

The farmer replied, "Maybe so, maybe not. We'll see."

Officers from the army arrived in town to recruit all the able-bodied young men for the war. They left behind the injured boy. "This is the best news I could have wished for!" the farmer's wife exclaimed.

The farmer replied, "Maybe so, maybe not. We'll see."

What's in my bag?

A shoulder bag or handbag full of unnecessary items is nothing but a weight. Bullet only what you need in it and give your shoulder a rest.

○
○
○
○
○
○
○
○
○
○
○
○
○
○
○

○
○
○
○
○
○
○
○
○
○
○
○
○
○
○

Place items that you occasionally want into a separate clear packet—add this to your bag when required.

～ My outfits ～

Bullet clothing combinations to create your favorite oufits for any occasion in advance, to save thinking when you are in a rush.

○   ○

○   ○

○   ○

My piggy bank

Date / /

Money buys me tickets,
not culture

Me-time

"Adventure is worthwhile in itself" —Amelia Earhart

Monthly me

"Start by doing what is necessary; then do what's possible; and suddenly you are doing the impossible" —Francis of Assisi

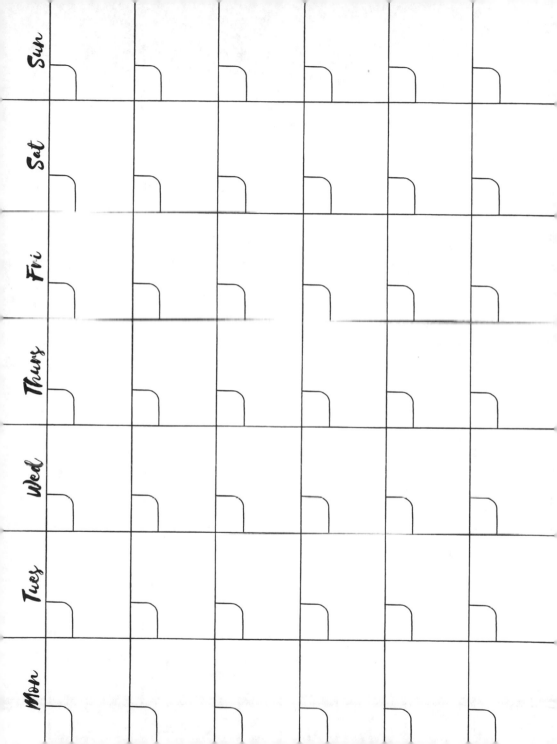

Task tracker

Date	Type	Status	Task
		○	
		○	
		○	
		○	
		○	
		○	
		○	
		○	
		○	
		○	
		○	
		○	
		○	
		○	
		○	
		○	
		○	
		○	
		○	
		○	
		○	
		○	
		○	

"While others prayed for the good time coming, I worked for it" —Victoria Woodhull

Organizing my time

We all feel short on time, but we all waste it too. Using it for true enjoyment is not waste. Frittering it away for no gain is regretful.
To organize your time, note the things of little value that you are doing, such as watching excessive television or socializing with people you don't like:

○
○
○
○

Stop procrastinating by over-thinking the future or past. What can you do _now_ that's beneficial to you?

○
○
○
○
○

"Time stays long enough for those who make use of it" —Leonardo da Vinci

Spontaneous ideas

Add spontaneity to your spare moments. Bullet a hitlist of venues, events and public places to get around to visiting— particularly any local to you. When a free hour strikes, use it, be spontaneous, check them out.

Flowers for me

Write your goals on the image.
Color it in as you achieve them.

113

Plan to attract

Planning a day has its obvious practical uses. However, it is also an effective way of visualizing for success. Try it when facing a difficult day that you wish to go well. Create the day exactly as you want it to happen:

"Life is largely a matter of expectation" —Horace

❀ Refresh myself

Three new things I am grateful for:
- ○ ....
- ○ ....
- ○ ....

Two life areas I am improving:
- ○ ....
- ○ ....

Three new affirmations or beliefs:
- ○ ....
- ○ ....
- ○ ....

Two current goals:
- ○ ....
- ○ ....

One current challenge:
- ○ ....

"The beginning is always today"
—Mary Wollstonecraft

My piggy bank

Date / /

"Nothing is worth more than this day"
—Johann Wolfgang von Goethe

Me-time

"Find ecstasy in life; the mere sense of living is joy enough" —Emily Dickinson

Monthly me

"Beware the barrenness of a busy life"

—Socrates

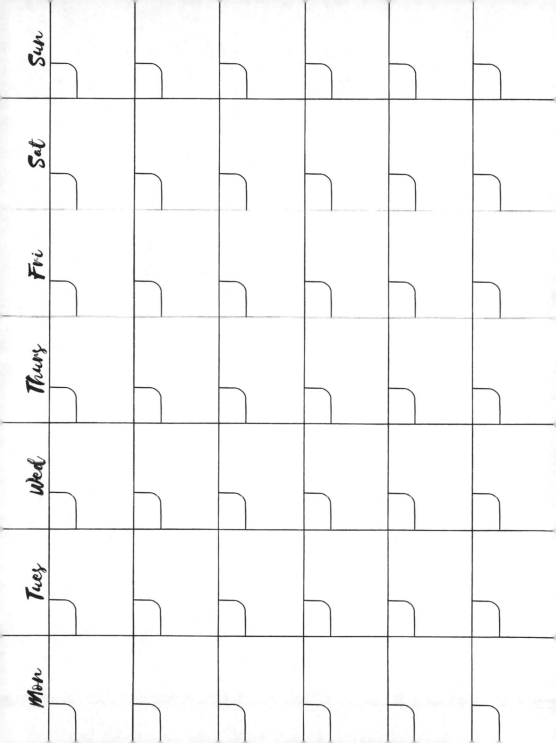

Task tracker

Date	Type	Status	Task
		○	
		○	
		○	
		○	
		○	
		○	
		○	
		○	
		○	
		○	
		○	
		○	
		○	
		○	
		○	
		○	
		○	
		○	
		○	
		○	
		○	
		○	
		○	

"A minute's success pays the
failure of years" —Robert Browning

♡ Cherished memories ♡

Keep images to reflect on with fondness. Bullet happy memories and paste in photographs of loved ones, pets or places.

"Memory is the diary we all carry about with us" —Oscar Wilde

My bucket list

Create a bucket list of 50 things you would like to do in life: places to explore, specific experiences or achievements to aim for.

- ○
- ○
- ○
- ○
- ○
- ○
- ○
- ○
- ○
- ○
- ○
- ○

- ○
- ○
- ○
- ○
- ○
- ○
- ○
- ○
- ○
- ○
- ○
- ○

○

○

○

○

○

○

○

○

○

○

○

○

○

○

○

○

○

○

○

○

○

○

○

○

Is there one you can cross off this month?
What are you waiting for?

～ My dripping tap ～

Now and then we notice little things in our surroundings or routine that we would benefit from altering, but that aren't urgent enough for us to get around to doing. For instance, an email list to unsubscribe from, a cable TV plan we're paying too much for, or a file of papers to throw out. These add up and become the dripping taps in our lives. Bullet your dripping taps whenever you encounter them. When you have a positive moment, fix one, not as a chore but as a positive act of kindness to yourself.

- ○
- ○
- ○
- ○
- ○
- ○
- ○
- ○

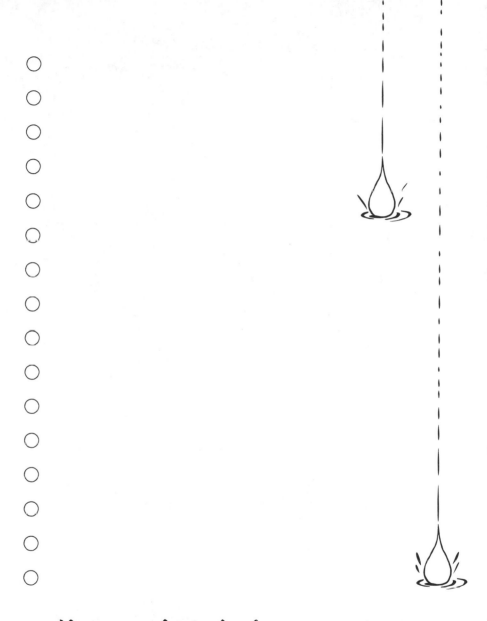

- ○
- ○
- ○
- ○
- ○
- ○
- ○
- ○
- ○
- ○
- ○
- ○
- ○
- ○
- ○
- ○

"What is right to be done cannot be done too soon" —Jane Austen

My piggy bank

Date / /

Money buys me acquaintances,
not friends

Me-time

"Life must be lived as play" —Plato

Monthly me

"Housekeeping ain't no joke"

—Louisa May Alcott

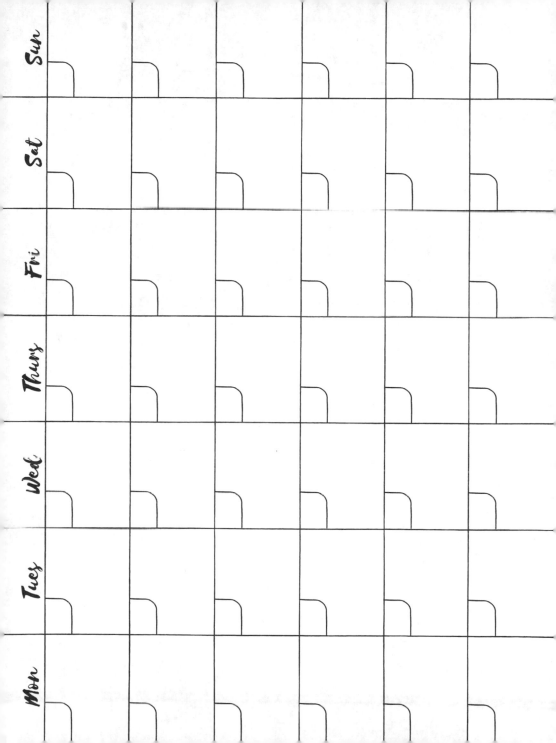

Task tracker

Date	Type	Status	Task
		○	
		○	
		○	
		○	
		○	
		○	
		○	
		○	
		○	
		○	
		○	
		○	
		○	
		○	
		○	
		○	
		○	
		○	
		○	
		○	
		○	
		○	
		○	

"Whoever is happy will make others happy too" —Anne Frank

 # Handy numbers

Bullet useful contact numbers: the dentist, hairdresser, florist, plumber, etc.—even if some are in your phone. Have them on hand to use and to pass on.

○
○
○
○
○
○
○
○
○
○
○
○
○
○
○
○
○

Supermarket

Avoid writing repeat shopping lists. Bullet all your regular items and occasional items here, once. When it's time to shop, use this as your checklist—simply place a pencil mark beside the items you need.

"No" Saying "no" is critical to getting organized. Notice occasions, places, people and purchases from which you do not receive a great deal of value or enjoyment, either altruistically or selfishly. Notice tasks you take on that are not your responsibility. Do this without judgment of yourself or others. It will offer you insight into where you're not being true to yourself. Begin to say "no" politely, without guilt, and start being led by your nature, which is where your positive energy exists. What can you say "no" to?

○
○
○
○
○
○
○
○
○
○
○

Passwords

Bullet your passwords. Redo old or bad choices. Create them from long-term memories and record them using abbreviated associations so only you can decipher them. For instance, if you once had a lorloise called **Speedy Gonzalez** and lived at **126 Orchard Drive**, create the password **SpeedyG126** but record it by abbreviated association such as **T7Trees–T7** signifying the first seven letters of **Speedy**'s name and **Trees** to jog **Orchard Drive** in your memory. If you wish, add false characters that you know are never in your passwords, e.g. **T744TrBBees**—knowing **BB** and **44** are meaningless. Your system will become second nature to you. Have at least five passwords and never use the most valuable (email, bank etc.) for general online sign-ups.

- ◯
- ◯
- ◯
- ◯
- ◯
- ◯

Skillful me

Advance your professional or hobby-based skills.
Bullet what to focus on learning next.

○

○

○

○

○

○

○

○

○

○

○

○

○

Search for an online tutorial as a staring point.

"I am still learning" —Michelangelo

✿ Refresh myself

Three new things I am grateful for:
○ ....
○ ....
○ ....

Two life areas I am improving:
○ ....
○ ....

Three new affirmations or beliefs:
○ ....
○ ....
○ ....

Two current goals:
○ ....
○ ....

One current challenge:
○ ....

"I want to be all that I am capable of becoming" —Katherine Mansfield

My piggy bank

Date / /

"Life is ours to be spent,
not to be saved" —D. H. Lawrence

"Faith in oneself is the best and safest course" —Michelangelo

Monthly me

"The future is purchased by the present"

—Samuel Johnson

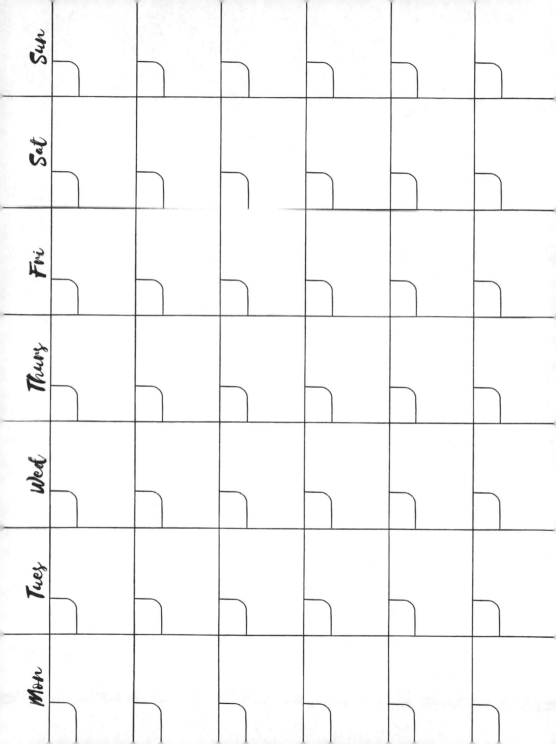

Task tracker

Date	Type	Status	Task
		○	
		○	
		○	
		○	
		○	
		○	
		○	
		○	
		○	
		○	
		○	
		○	
		○	
		○	
		○	
		○	
		○	
		○	
		○	
		○	
		○	
		○	
		○	
		○	

"Be as you wish to seem" —Socrates

— My must-dos —

Track your must-dos for a month.

	1	2	3	4	5	6	7	8	9	10	11	12	13

Are you keeping up those daily routines and the promises you've made to yourself?

14	15	16	17	18	19	20	21	22	23	24	25	26	27	28	29	30	31

My progress

Regardless of what we have or don't have, we feel happiest when we are progressing. Change happens; some goals come easy and others elude us but progress determines our sense of worth, and progress is always achievable.

Bullet your progress, from tiny accomplishments to large ones: a great day, a challenge attempted, a habit tweaked, an event attended, a project begun. Noticing your progress will lead to more.

○

"Be yourself.
Everyone else is
already taken"
—Oscar Wilde

My piggy bank

Date / /

**Money buys me lust,
not love**

Me-time

"Forever is composed of nows"

—Emily Dickinson

Monthly me

"Use the occasion, for it passes swiftly" —Ovid

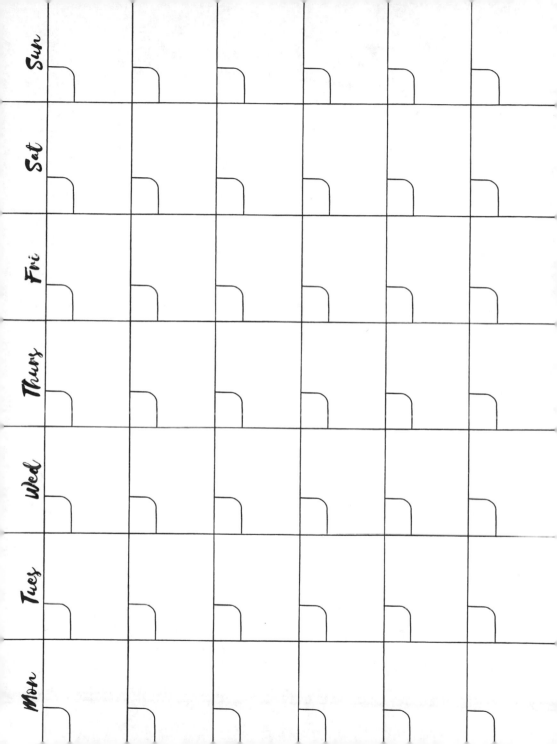

Task tracker

Date	Type	Status	Task
		○	
		○	
		○	
		○	
		○	
		○	
		○	
		○	
		○	
		○	
		○	
		○	
		○	
		○	
		○	
		○	
		○	
		○	
		○	
		○	
		○	
		○	

"I will prepare and some day my chance will come" —Abraham Lincoln

~ My inspirations ~

Gather sayings and quotations that are meaningful or uplifting to you:

"Words, like nature, half reveal and half conceal the soul within" —Alfred, Lord Tennyson

❀ Refresh myself

Three new things I am grateful for:

○ ....

○ ....

○ ....

Two life areas I am improving:

○ ....

○ ....

Three new affirmations or beliefs:

○ ....

○ ....

○ ....

Two current goals:

○ ....

○ ....

One current challenge:

○ ....

"Tomorrow is always fresh, with no mistakes in it" —Lucy Maud Montgomery

My piggy bank

Date / /

"Getting and spending, we lay
waste our powers" —William Wordsworth

Me-time

"*The energy of the mind is the essence of life*" —Aristotle

Wheel of balance

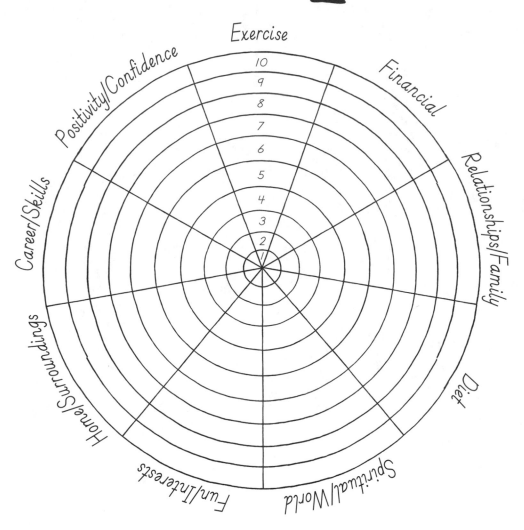

Refresh your Wheel of balance.

An ounce of practice is worth a ton of theory.

The following pages provide 52 weekly templates for you to use however you choose. During busy weeks you may wish to organize your schedule. At other times, you can use the space to develop affirmations, projects, gratitude lists, vision boards, projects, or anything else of benefit to you. Each week, keep in mind your key goals, challenges and lifestyle improvements. Pursue what works for you and your time. Be gorgeously organized to create the life you want.

week 1

m

t

w

t

f

sa

su

Top goal: ....

add date

add month

A fresh challenge: ....

Top goal: ....

m

t

w

t

f

sa

su

A self-care activity: ....

week 3

Top goal: ....

m

t

w

t

f

sa

su

I am grateful for: ....

Top goal: ....

m

t

w

t

f

sa

su

An affirmation: ....

week 5

m

t

w

t

f

sa

su

Top goal: ....

Fix my dripping tap: ....

Top goal: ....

m

t

w

t

f

sa

su

Life area to focus on: ....

week 7

m

t

w

t

f

sa

su

Top goal:..

To help my piggy bank:..

Top goal: ....

m

t

w

t

f

sa

su

A habit to keep: ....

week 9

m

t

w

t

f

sa

su

Top goal: ....

A spontaneous activity: ....

Top goal: ....

m

t

w

t

f

sa

su

Something to enjoy: ....

week 11

Top goal: ....

m

t

w

t

f

sa

su

Say "no" to: ....

Top goal: ....

m

t

w

t

f

sa

su

I want: ....

week 13

m

t

w

t

f

sa

su

Top goal: ....

Exercise target: ....

Top goal: ....

week 14

m
t
w
t
f
sa
su

Dietary improvement: ....

Top goal: ....

m

t

w

t

f

sa

su

A positive belief: ....

Top goal:..

m

t

w

t

f

sa

su

A skill to advance:...

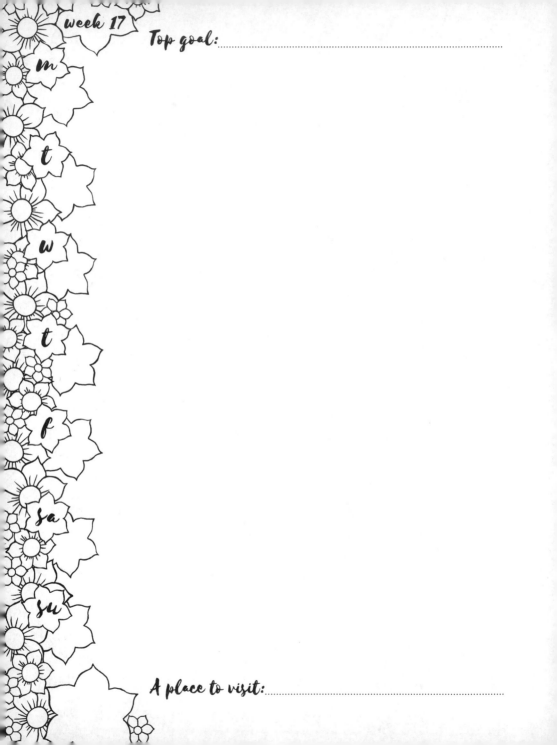

week 17

Top goal:...

m

t

w

t

f

sa

su

A place to visit:...

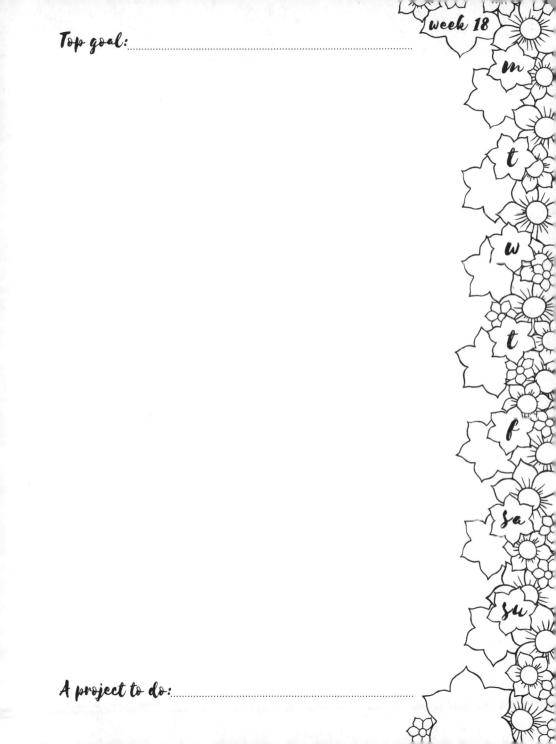

Top goal: ....

week 18

m

t

w

t

f

sa

su

A project to do: ....

week 19

Top goal: ....

m

t

w

t

f

sa

su

Pursue my interest: ....

Top goal: ....

m

t

w

t

f

sa

su

Delegate this: ....

m

t

w

t

f

sa

su

Top goal:..

I wish to attract:..

Top goal: ....

m

t

w

t

f

sa

su

Notice progress: ....

week 23

Top goal: ....

m

t

w

t

f

sa

su

Give to others by: ....

Top goal: ....

m

t

w

t

f

sa

su

Create more time by: ....

week 25

m

t

w

t

f

sa

su

Top goal:...

A home improvement:...

Top goal: ....

m

t

w

t

f

sa

su

Cross this off my Bucket list: ....

Top goal: ....

m

t

w

t

f

sa

su

Revisit my Personal mission statement.

Top goal: ....

m

t

w

t

f

sa

su

Revisit my Wheel of balance.

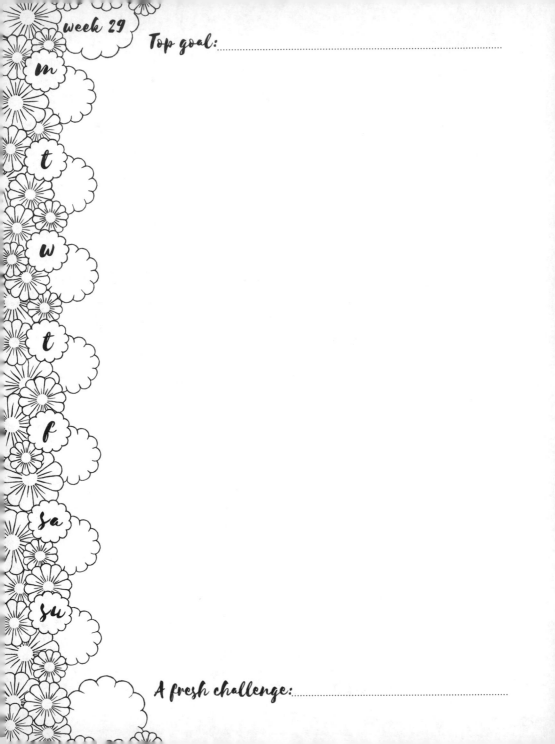

week 29

m

t

w

t

f

sa

su

Top goal: ....

A fresh challenge: ....

Top goal:

m

t

w

t

f

sa

su

A self-care activity:

week 31

Top goal: ....

m

t

w

t

f

sa

su

I am grateful for: ....

Top goal: ....

m

t

w

t

f

sa

su

An affirmation: ....

week 33

Top goal: ....

m

t

w

t

f

sa

su

Fix my dripping tap: ....

Top goal: ....

m

t

w

t

f

sa

su

Life area to focus on: ....

week 35

Top goal: ....

m

t

w

t

f

sa

su

To help my piggy bank: ....

Top goal:

m

t

w

t

f

sa

su

A habit to keep:

week 37

m

t

w

t

f

sa

su

Top goal:...

A spontaneous activity:...

Top goal: ....

m

t

w

t

f

sa

su

Something to enjoy: ....

week 39

Top goal:...

m

t

w

t

f

sa

su

Say "no" to:...

Top goal: ....

m

t

w

t

f

sa

su

I want: ....

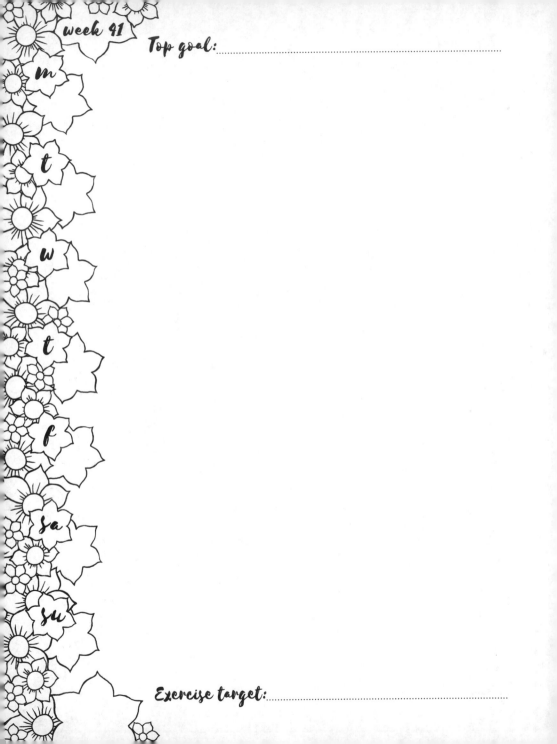

week 41

m

t

w

t

f

sa

su

Top goal:...

Exercise target:...

Top goal: ....

m

t

w

t

f

sa

su

Dietary improvement: ....

week 43

Top goal: ....

m

t

w

t

f

sa

su

A positive belief: ....

Top goal: ....

m

t

w

t

f

sa

su

A skill to advance: ....

week 45

Top goal:...

m

t

w

t

f

sa

su

A place to visit:..

Top goal: ....

m

t

w

t

f

sa

su

A project to do: ....

week 47

Top goal: ....

m

t

w

t

f

sa

su

Pursue my interest: ....

Top goal: ....

m

t

w

t

f

sa

su

Delegate this: ....

week 49

Top goal: ....

m

t

w

t

f

sa

su

I wish to attract: ....

Top goal:

m

t

w

t

f

sa

su

Notice progress:

week 51

m

t

w

t

f

sa

su

Top goal:...

Give to others by:...

Top goal: ....

m

t

w

t

f

sa

su

Create more time by: ....

My friends' addresses

"The only way to have a friend
is to be one" —Raplh Waldo Emerson

"'Stay' is a charming word in a friend's vocabulary" —Louisa May Alcott

"My best friend is the one who brings out the best in me" —Henry Ford

"Your friend is your needs answered" —Khalil Gibran

"*Friendship is a sheltering tree*"

—Samuel Taylor Coleridge

"Friendships are discovered rather than made" —Harriet Beecher Stowe

"*A friend is a gift you give yourself*"

—*Robert Louis Stevenson*

One-year glance

m	t	w	t	f	sa	su

m	t	w	t	f	sa	su

m	t	w	t	f	sa	su

m	t	w	t	f	sa	su

m	t	w	t	f	sa	su

m	t	w	t	f	sa	su

Insert months and dates.

m	t	w	t	f	sa	su

m	t	w	t	f	sa	su

m	t	w	t	f	sa	su

m	t	w	t	f	sa	su

m	t	w	t	f	sa	su

m	t	w	t	f	sa	su

Glue an envelope here to store any loose bits and pieces that you wish to keep in your *Little Bullet Book*.

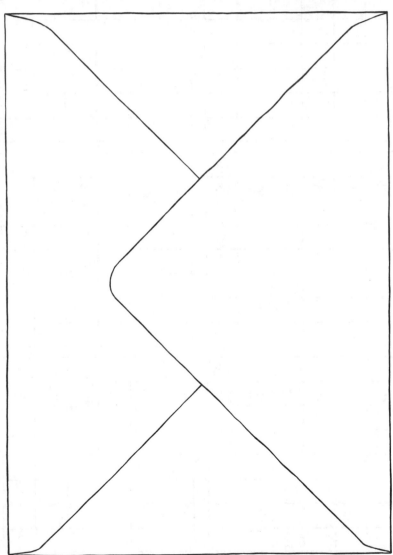